EX CATHEDRA

XXIX

PETER JOANNIDES

Printed in the United States of America

First Printing, 2020

ISBN 978-1-7324338-1-6

www.PetroulisI@gmail.com

ALSO BY PETER JOANNIDES

Amán Amán!

Ex Cathedras (IX-XV)

More Ex Cathedras (XVI-XXII)

Ex Cathedra XXIII

Ex Cathedra XXIV

Ex Cathedra XXV

Ex Cathedra XXVI

Ex Cathedra XXVII

Ex Cathedra XXVIII

Author's Note

This is the latest in the series of **Ex Cathedras** begun in 1972.

The **Ex Cathedras (IX—XXVIII)** preceding this one had some inconsistencies with the punctuations of titles and foreign words—movies, books, newspapers, songs, articles, etc. Sometimes they were bolded; other times quotation marks were used. I have tried to rectify this by second printings which I hoped would add a measure of conformity, and believe I have mostly succeeded.

In this **Ex Cathedra**, and possibly others to follow (should I be given any extra lease on life), I shall adopt the following guidelines: Bona-fide books will be bolded. Movies, newspapers, songs, articles, etc. will be set off by quotation marks. Transliterated words in Greek (other than geographical names) will be bolded and for polysyllabic ones an acute diacritical mark will be used to indicate stress. Words in other languages, if any, will conform to the conventions of those languages.

Bolding may also be used for transliterated words of foreign languages and, along with font size, for special emphasis.

I would like to take this occasion, while I am still able, to rectify an omission that was unfortunately not included in the list of acknowledgements to be found at the end of Volume 3 of **Amán Amán!** And that is the name of Wayne Hamm, who was extremely helpful, especially regarding the early stages of my major work.

Dr. Hamm, who died at the untimely age of 42, was the closest thing to a critical literary genius that I have ever had, personally, the privilege to know.

Peter Joannides

November 01, 2020

Ex Cathedra

29th
Encyclical

von Herrn Doktor Professor Peter Joannides

1

As soon as I become The Planetary Dictator, Steve Raichlen will be ordered to immediately report to my culinary staff.

2

Senator Orrin Hatch is still slimy, but in a sort of special, unobvious, unimmediate way.

3

The elder Russell wasn't quite fair to the later Wittgenstein.

The germ of the **Investigations** was already pre-envisaged in the **Tractatus** 4.002: "The silent adjustments to understand colloquial language are enormously complicated."

4

One of the little frustrations of life: pistachios that are openable (but at the risk of separated nails and painful fingers), but not easily openable.

5

I still can't forgive Ralph Nader (with a little help from the Gang of Five) for throwing the election to Bush.

(Just as I can't Jill Stein for probably throwing it to you-know-who.)

Our whole recent American history might be quite different now.

This is what happens when you don't think before you act.

6

If a sentence **flows**, it doesn't matter if it is grammatically incorrect.

7

To those who would say something disparaging about my non-participation:

I am not a cipher.

8

I'm mellowing and mellowing. Some people I strongly disliked in the past, I don't dislike all that much anymore.

(Some I'm beginning to actually like; for example, the actor George C. Scott.)

9

What is it with me and **exactness**?

Clock Time

Preparation of Food

Spelling and Punctuation

Volume

Lighting

Duration

Amount

Time of Day

Removal of the Slightest Spots in the Wrong Places

Symmetry

Order

. . .

10

Killing animals is one thing; torturing them is quite another.

11

After all, my mother was a communist sympathizer. What else did you expect me to turn out to be but a leaner to the left.

 # 11

It pains me, however, to think how it would have pained her to know the truth about Stalin.

13

What happened to the days when I had to rush to the library to look all sorts of things up, rummage around in the stacks, make frantic calls to colleagues and friends, consult dictionaries, geographies, usage manuals, thesauruses…

When now all I have to do is ask God.

(Google)

14

Ichthyologists, entomologists, herpetologists, mammalogists… assure us of the interdependence of animal species—including sharks, snakes, crocodiles, jellyfish, insects—and talk about food chains, pollinations, and the importance of natural balances.

And no doubt they're right.

But I still have my fears, dislikes, and aversions.

15

We live in two very different worlds, those of wakefulness and those of dreams, whose connection is a very great and insoluble mystery.

 # 15

Don't talk to me about wires and brain scans and scientifically monitored measurements of electrical impulses and correspondences… and other irrelevancies.

"Wakefulness" trying to subsume what is unsubsumable and rearing its presumptuous head.

17

The directions of our lives so often hang by a thread.

18

When I become The Planetary Dictator, Neil deGrasse Tyson and George Hiscock will be my spokesmen.

They can take turns relieving one another.

19

I've always had good feelings about Ehud Barak.

20

"99% of your Readers won't even notice such a minor and trivial error."

It doesn't matter. It is still wrong. And it should be fixed.

21

All these many years, I've hardly been interested in politics.

Until now.

22

I love that rubbery feel about **haloúmi**.

23

"I'll Buy That Dream"

Not a bad song, pleasant and soothing. (With all its many singers and versions.) But as soon as I hear "autogyro," I wince.

24

I once learned the hard way not to desert a handball partner that I had been winning doubles tournaments with, so that I could team up with someone who had a sort of national singles reputation and would be a sure-fire way of winning.

Only to be defeated in the finals (I believe 11-10 in the tiebreaker) by that same old partner who had found someone else to play with.

25

Doubles is not the same as singles.

(The Monster Team of Hershkowitz and Jacobs could probably be taken by Sloan and Collins.)

26

Some of those jokes in “The New Yorker” are a bit too subtle for me.

27

Eulogies are insidious. They suck you in, and then you have to suck yourself out.

28

Jeff Bezos

See **Ex Cathedra XVII # 135**.

29

I'd hate to be the captain of a nuclear-powered aircraft carrier or submarine. The only way I can see it is that he would have to in some way compartmentalize the hours of his day so that he would have some surcease from the awesomeness of his responsibilities.

30

What our President needs is to go through some terrible illness or severe physical crisis and then somehow be delivered from it.

And then to have an epiphany.

I think it would make a man out of him.

It might even make him a Democrat.

31

The least bit of gristle on my meat was (and is) always an absolute no-no for me.

32

There's something fascinating about a remote.

How one can go from instantly shutting down an asshole to mouth-watering recipes to memorable old films to round-table discussions/analyses to weather warnings to congressional hearings to a baseball game to a travelogue…

And all at the flick of a finger.

33

Kant: Protagoras systematized.

34

I can no longer ever dine with the Queen of England.

As I think I would need a bib; and I'm sure it would never be allowed.

35

I’m leaning toward this proclamation:

Sour cream has it over yogurt.

36

Baked potato, the other of the Triumvirate along with **tempura** and fried **haloúmi**, that I would like to be served piping hot (with a dollop of butter), piece by piece, bit by bit, at my receiving table.

37

If I had had a little more **chutzpah**, my work would probably have been successfully published by now.

38

Enormous swaths of ocean gyres full of refuse, garbage, plastics…

What are we to do now with Zarathustra’s “One must be a sea, to receive a polluted stream without becoming defiled”?

39

It’s hard to judge oneself.

40

That’s all I ever wanted out of this life: to win the Big Lotto, to be awarded the Nobel Prize for Literature, and to be The Planetary Dictator.

41

I wonder why I dislike Joseph Rosendo so much.

Is it that he reminds me of my former me?

42

I like apple sauce a lot better than apples.

43

Today is March 7, 2019

Ex Cathedra XXIV # 137

Ex Cathedra XXV # 128

Ex Cathedra XXVI # 175

ALL FIXED!

44

The translation of my work to Greek would require collaboration between a Greek-**American** well versed in Greek and an American-**Greek** well versed in American. (Mainly the latter.)

Not the one without the other.

44

The situation **really** gets complicated when talking about translations to **other** languages.

46

Habits and artifacts that were in full-fledged practice and use just a few years ago, two years ago, even a year ago—now fading into fallowness and obscurity.

47

There's quite a streak of Silas Marner in me, I'm sorry to say.

48

I don’t like middlemen.

I suppose they serve some sort of positive function.

But I still don’t like the whole idea of them.

 # 48

Just substitute “lobbyists” and “literary agents” for “middlemen.”

50

I wonder who has **really** traveled more—me or Hillary.

51

The only **real** Miss Marple is Margaret Rutherford.

52

I think I could begin to understand the mind and soul of a political assassin.

53

Just because animals can't tell you they're in a lot of pain doesn't mean they're not in a lot of pain.

54

I'm definitely a lowbrow when it comes to music, art, theater…

Not so, with food, cinema, locale…

55

“Height” should be spelled “heighth.”

56

My work was meant for an educated—but not a professorial—audience.

57

When the oceans themselves get polluted, it seems to me we're nearing the end of the line.

58

I'm not sure I want to deal with a publisher who requires an agent for submissions.

59

I hadn't realized there are so many super-intelligent women out there.

60

Republican Senator Richard Lugar of Indiana was a good man.

61

I wonder how many frantically switch from TV channel to channel, **anything** to avoid those asinine commercials.

62

What I love about (and am indebted to) Logan Pearsall Smith, is that I can, at any time and at my discretion, change the subject.

(Not only for apothegms, but for sustained disquisitions as well.)

63

We've had Bill Maher all this time.

Now we also have Trevor Noah.

64

I can’t think fast enough to argue.

But later, after I’ve reviewed what I could have said and should have said, I would have torn my opponent to shreds.

65

My father was **scholastikós**.

He would repeat the very same thing over and over again to make sure everybody got it.

I am my father's son.

66

There's something fatuous about the narrator of a documentary taking a picture of the "natives" with the full knowledge that someone else is taking a picture of him (so nauseatingly and hammily proud of himself) taking a picture.

67

A documentary with Joseph Rosendo is all about Joseph Rosendo.

68

Except for a few notable examples, once you read a book you hardly ever go back to it.

69

GEMS

Robert Benchley sending his editor a telegram from Venice:

"Streets full of water. Please advise."

Dorothy Parker asked why she had not delivered her copy in time:

"Tell him I've been too fucking busy—or vice versa."

70

Morpheus, my now favorite god and bosom companion.

71

Space junk: Aside from its physical dangers, what a loathsome and celestial aesthetic tragedy.

72

Where do I find my privacy any longer? Inside my unvoiced mind?

And even that, so I hear, is subject to disclosure.

73

I can’t bear looking at anything crooked, not even the least bit crooked.

74

Kids: sometimes I can’t stand those pesky little plaguey annoying irksome obnoxious in-your-face dynamos.

75

Dating back to the old old days, whenever I want to check whether a month has 31 or 30 days, I still do so by counting my knuckles.

76

Given all the intersections, junctions, crossings, latticeworks of my existence, I sometimes wonder about all the varied lifetimes I might have led.

77

Although I know that they are for the most part practical and necessary, still, recordings that give off the aura of originals have somehow always bothered me.

78

I remember Captain Yianni Paksimadis and his beloved **“Antiópi,”** and if he said it to me once, he said it a score of times (roughly, as well as I can recall it): “**ke ótan o Cháros o íthios tha perási, k’aftón na ton kerásis!**” (“and when the Grim Reaper himself should come by, treat **him** to a drink as well!”).

79

Oh if only what would happen to “our” President is what happened to Ebenezer Scrooge.

So many foods that are supposedly so good for you are like eating hay.

81

Why has it taken so long for me to learn this:

"So often fixing one thing means unfixing another"?

82

Lately, I've been thinking about the number of distinguishable colors and shades of colors that I had put at about 3,000 in my Aesthetic Section in **Aman Aman!**

Now, with the help of Maya, I'm beginning to suspect that that may have been far too conservative a figure.

Sometimes one wants to write something that he ought to be writing.

But he refrains for fear that it might offend a dear and living friend.

Even though all of us, including the dear and living friend, will soon be gone.

But such is the nature of empathy and forbearance.

84

So many old old memories, but hardly anyone around anymore to share.

85

I should have been born into the world of Section XVI in **Aman Aman!**

I **resent** not having been so.

86

It must be nice to be a paleontologist and have a clear and positive and demarcated area of interest and responsibility, and be more or less absolved of all other constraints.

87

Errol Flynn

Talk about burning the candle at both ends!

Some of my favorite songs:

"South of the Border"
"Amapola"
"Elmer's Tune"
"Chattanooga Choo Choo"
"Dance Ballerina Dance"
"Green Eyes"
"Heartaches"
"Mas (More)"
"La Vie en Rose"
"Don't Sit Under the Apple Tree"
"Music Makes Me"
"The Waiter and the Porter and the Upstairs Maid"
"Good Morning, Mr. Walker"
"Weisse Rosen aus Athen"
"Jeepers Creepers"
"Flat Foot Floogie"
"Never on Sunday"

89

There are more good people than bad.

God help us if the proportion should ever change!

90

In my world, there are no speechwriters.

91

“Our” President

The Greek word for parrot is **papagálos**.

92

To Publishers

Fuck you and your “fit”s.

93

It is uncivilized to dine at 5 PM.

In every hospital, rehab center, etc. there will always be at least one "Javert" nurse.

A "Javert" nurse is unswerving in her devotion to her duties, follows the rules to the letter and the nth degree, admits of no exceptions or bending of the rules, and has hardly the slightest trace of empathy, sympathy, or the smallest consideration for the sufferings and needs of her patients.

A "Javert" nurse might as well be a robot.

95

Ah to be a billionaire and have a backscratcher at your beck and call 24/7.

96

Overcooked eggs are an abomination.

97

You can only owe so much suffering and pain to your kids.

98

Not having read it, and now having been in a rehabilitation facility, I now know all there is to know about Dante’s **Inferno** and its seven tiers.

99

I can’t think of anything more exciting than to be masturbated by a nurse because the doctor ordered a sample of semen.

100

We owe Joyce the general idea of stream-of-consciousness (a not insignificant debt), but not **necessarily** much else.

101

I hear “quiche” and I immediately go into nausea mode.

102

We make choices all the time; we just can’t help making the choices that we make.

103

The three passions of my life: completing **Aman Aman!**, travel, and handball.

Handball: I've had some Great Wins; and some Great Losses.

105

The difference between a Greek-American and a real Greek is he who knows the Greek word for "thumb."

What's wrong with scientists! Why can't they invent a Foley, hardly noticeable and miniaturized and worn on the body like any other piece of apparel, and involved in a chemical alteration that will relieve one from urinating and also from emptying. Permanent freedom.

And also one for BM's.

All the eating and drinking without ever having to pee or defecate.

107

Of all times—personal time, current time, historical time, geologic time, astronomic time—the real-est of all is personal time.

108

I find everything interesting, except pain.

109

It is morally wrong and I suspect unhealthy to eat food that doesn't taste good.

110

I've made some put-down and smart-alec and self-serving remarks about certain people, that I now ruefully regret.

111

Just think of it: On any given day, millions flying overhead encased in flying machines, millions laboring, millions driving, millions touristing, millions celebrating, millions arguing, copulating, contracting diseases, convalescing, suffering accidents, cheering athletic events, joking, contemplating suicide, sleeping, eating, laughing, being born, dying.

112

Only at the Waffle House is bacon prepared as it should be prepared: stiff, snap, and crinkly.

113

Nearly everyone has some sort of job.

I've often wondered what my job exactly is.

114

So many: a lot of wind.

115

Are there as many sounds and tones as there are words? And as many ways of putting them together?

And what about colors and tastes?

Unfortunately, not so with smells.

You'd have to be a dog.

116

I remember that day I took Pop up in a Piper Cub, and we flew all over Hampton Roads, with me at the controls.

I still can’t believe I actually did this.

117

I don't know if pilots realize this, but they're at the mercy of their machines.

118

It's eerie how I resemble the habits and dispositions of my father in many ways.

119

Here I am now trapped in my dysfunctional body. Not an easy thing to accept.

120

Every once in a while, you come across a good doctor.

121

When an old man starts going downhill, he goes fast.

122

Somehow, I feel that everything I've written is golden and carved in stone.

123

How dated all the turmoil of current events will one day seem.

124

How I dislike a lemon or lime that half-heartedly dribbles when you pinch it.

125

In more or less recent times, oh how many heads of state, political opponents, government thorns, protest leaders, have been ruthlessly mercilessly gunned down.

126

Once upon a time, the 40's were the forefront of time.

Just about every Republican **AND** every Democrat toes the Party line.

It's embarrassing.

128

Every once in a while, the thought comes startlingly to mind: My God, if she is still amongst the living, she must be in her 80's by now!

129

Nona wasted her life on me.

She was eminently worthy of being a companion to a Minister, a Head of State, an Entrepreneur, a Captain of Industry…

I tried to create what I thought would be something that was momentous and unprecedented, and so would justify her sacrifice, but I had neither the means nor the personality and capability to promote it.

130

Adam Gopnik

No one could possibly know so much about so much.

131

The truth is:

I've never been too enamored of highbrow music.

Just about any form of it.

 # 131

In fact, I think it shares some of the faults and foibles of Painting and Higher Art. (See **Aman Aman!**, Vol. 3, Sec. XXVI, Second and Third Digressions, pp. 1414—1419.)

133

I have a special relationship with triple-cream brie.

134

To really enjoy a culinary delicacy, you must not have it for a while.

Therefore, it would seem that the rewarding thing to do is to **rotate** a goodly number of delicacies.

135

I don’t know why I identify with Virginia Woolf and her life and tragic end, but the fact is I do, and that I don’t remotely know why.

Technological miracles had for the asking, and I had no idea.

137

For the most part:

Dictators have a meteoric rise, a glorious acme, and an ignominious end.

Sort of like a parabolic clockwork.

138

How glib the advice of others who are not in the same torment.

139

Not so long ago, I said that urologists were a sorry crew.

Now, it has grown into outright contempt.

140

Frank Capra

A remarkable man. Who else could have captured the **good** soul of America so well.

141

This is my second go-round with the Mayo Clinic.

I have every right and desire to spit the severest curses and venom at the Mayo Clinic.

This morning I woke up with sudden images of Father Flanagan (Spencer Tracy), Mickey Rooney, and “Boys Town.” Very pronounced images and overwhelming everything else. (I even remember how enthused about the movie mama was.)

And one thing led to another, and there were suddenly the Andy Hardy films with Judge Lewis Stone and “man-to-man” talks and Aunt Milly and luscious Ann Rutherford.

How can one ever forget Mickey Rooney, even as one can’t ever forget Carmen Miranda.

143

Sometimes all it takes to correct a computer problem is the jiggle of a wire.

But what good is it for the one who doesn't know which wire to jiggle?

144

I find it quite fascinating that native speakers so fluidly unthinkingly instantiate the rules of grammar.

This is the sort of problem that probably would have intrigued Bertrand Russell:

Can we be **Absolutely Certain** that the refrigerator light is turned off when we close the refrigerator door?

146

I never thought it would come to this:

Often, when I want to phone someone, I now first have to be cleared by hard, metallic, disembodied voices.

And their predictable and irritating preamble, "If this is an emergency, please hang up and dial 911."

147

I don't like writers who bandy about numerous allusions to make sure you realize what a submerged-iceberg fund of knowledge, reading, and education they're possessed of.

(**How** it is done is important.)

I've done this myself.

But it's the difference between a short article (apt to be the more embarrassing) and a longer work that, by its very nature, has to be more revealing.

148

What I miss most of all is sitting in my front yard under the beneficent Florida spring and fall sunlight with a glass of red wine and maybe a cigar.

149

I think I would be judged by most to be a fairly decent individual. And I am.

But all the crazy, atrocious, depraved, dissolute, dishonorable, cowardly, imbecilic things I've done in my lifetime, you wouldn't believe.

150

The people who adore paintings are like those who see the Emperor's clothes.

151

I don’t have much truck with those self-congratulating (science-fiction?) films whose plots and sub-plots are so intricate and convoluted-entangled-interstitched that it takes a trendy nerdy genius to figure out what is going on.

Thanks, but no-thanks.

Please, don’t bother to explain.

Not long ago I read about some illegal immigrants who were found locked in a railroad box car and had perished.

I cannot get out of my mind the terrible suffering they must have endured.

153

A Documentary on the Life of George Orwell

Not only do we have an actor playing the part of George Orwell, but on top of that we're shown some tinselly home movies of the bogus George Orwell along with George Orwell's bogus wife playing with their bogus dog.

It is tasteless, phony, and lying stunts like this that bring dishonor to the whole acting profession.

154

It is comforting to know there is the Truth, even though we may never know it, or even **can** ever know it.

155

Sometimes the most honorable thing to do is to commit suicide.

156

Sometimes I can't remember many of the details I wrote so passionately about so many years ago.

In fact, sometimes I can't even identify certain individuals I wrote about so many years ago.

157

Nietzsche was absolutely right.

Modern Medicine sometimes works against his sage advice.

So many, after a life of vigor and excitement, have such terrible and woeful endings.

159

Did you ever stop to think that dipping buttered bread into an olive oil and vinegar mix could be a sort of meal in itself?

160

How it pierces to know there are things I will never again do.

Like having a drink and elegant meal in the dining car of the Amtrak train from L.A. to Seattle and watch the rolling Pacific scenery pass by.

161

I have very fond memories of “Cream of Wheat”s black man with the white chef’s hat and of Aunt Jemima.

(I guess Neil deGrasse Tyson can’t be right about everything.)

162

Rule of thumb for murder mysteries: The least likely suspect to be the murderer, the one you hardly ever give a second thought to—is the one.

163

I never saw so many deplorable boat handlers all in one place before.

164

Tearing down all those old statues is a bit puerile and ridiculous.

165

When my Atlas is lying around unused for a while, I want it to rest on a map with an adjacent body of ocean or sea water.

No inland map for me.

Americans, especially soldiers, take orders. They would obey an order to decimate a whole population.

Not that others wouldn't do the same thing.

The order-givers: they are the problem.

167

Oysters: I’ll take ’em anyway I can get ’em—raw, fried, baked, smoked…

168

There is something about the young (no matter how brilliant) that somehow withholds them from understanding the old.

(I suppose Eliot and his “Prufrock” is an exception.)

169

The learning and exposure of a young child die hard.

170

It’s taking less and less time for me to become bored with something or someone that I was very enthusiastic about not so very long ago.

171

That's me: constantly drowning in a cup of water.

172

I'd like to know who started the fire in Smyrna in 1922?

173

Could there be beings for whom our time-lapse would be their norm?

174

I've always been terrified of leprosy.

175

I wish I could apologize to long-gone Dana Andrews.

He was mostly right; and I was mostly wrong.

Senator and Vice-Presidential pick Kamala Harris: **kamomatoú** (Google Translate and **Divry's**: a lady full of "airs and graces," "carryings on," "affectations").

177

I wonder what would have happened had I listened to mama and gone to Harvard instead of Cornell? (It would have been Willard Van Orman Quine instead of Max Black and Li'l Abner clone Norman Malcolm.)

No Ninetta, no Nona, no Maya, no Jim and Nancy, no George, no University of Maryland, no Florida, nothing I am familiar with. Eliot's "what might have been" in stark and unarguable reality.

Maybe a life grandiose, maybe pedestrian, maybe tragic, maybe snuffed out.

Wouldn't it be interesting (like the All-Knower of Pierre Laplace) to know!

178

I am hoping that “our” President will lose the 2020 election by a landslide.

Just like McGovern.

Maybe this time that one lone state will turn out to be North Dakota.

179

The Coronavirus

I suppose it would be unnatural for me not to say something about this universal preoccupation.

What can I say?

A dystopian science-fiction fantasy suddenly become frighteningly **REAL**.

Frightening indeed! Aside from the Reaper's scythe that cuts away susceptible lives like overgrown grass, that old world that I've known all my life, that I took for granted, that old world of crowds and conviviality, **might never come back**.

What a difference between a prime-grade paper-thin prosciutto and an ordinary piece of ham!

181

Anyone who admires Eugene Debs (like Bernie Sanders) is on the right track.

182

The dermatologists tell me that I am now paying for my sins for having sat on the beach all those years worshipping the Almighty Sun.

“Death Wish” Films

Each one is worse than the one before it.

The first one wasn’t bad.

“Airport” Films

Each one is worse than the one before it.

The first one was good.

184

I don’t expect a doctor to have a bedside manner, but I do expect him to be somewhat civil, and reasonably polite and courteous.

 # 184

And not brusque and impatient and impertinent.

186

I think I have a two-dimensional mind, whatever that may mean to anyone, myself included.

187

"Numb" doesn't quite get it (translate) for "**mouthiasméno**."

188

I guess I've dabbled in just about everything sexual, but there are one or two things I missed—and I regret it.

189

You cannot **will** yourself to sleep, or if you can, I don't know how to do so.

It seems to me that willing yourself to sleep is an oxymoron and that—

Sleep is a form of grace.

O Prínkipas tis Ualías

(The Prince of Wales)

Helpless. Helpless I've always been. Have always depended on others to fill my so many needs:

to fix even the simplest mechanical structures that sometimes go wrong (I can hardly manage to turn a screw)—

to deal with even the simplest problems and requirements of a car—

to fix a flat tire—

to tend to mortgages, taxes, bank transactions, and assorted financial matters and responsibilities—

to select my very dress and clothes—

to do my laundry—

to provide the wherewithal to pursue my obsessions—

(continued)

to take up the grooming of yard and shrubs when I grudgingly would begin and then more or less abandon—

to help me when unable to retrace my way back from a destination, although I could find it going forward—

to be persuaded to abandon long-held but counter-productive habits—

to in later years be shown the most elementary ways and means of navigating a computer—

etc— etc—

192

Oktoberfest; Faliraki and Orfanithou Street, Rhodos

Why do they turn me off so, these slobbering,
maudlin, combative, dead-drunk idiots—
when I did do these very same things myself?

Talk about being protected from the goings-on in this world, I was a whole grown 31 years of age and in Morocco when I first saw (with a spurt of surprise and comprehension) an animal slaughtered and skinned on the spot.

194

For a while I couldn't get enough of **Karaghiózi**…and then it was airline disasters…and then it was biographies…

195

Any one of **several** minor happenings would have prevented the horrendous airline disaster on Tenerife.

Still, I continue to cross myself, and, of course, three times: **éla Christé ke Panayía, éla Christé ke Panayía, éla Christé ke Panayía**.

(Not so far removed, it seems am I, from prayer wheels and madrassas.)

197

I apologize to the full and undivided, unabbreviating Reader for all the repetitions.

198

I just realized I've made the very same preceding apology before.

My work should be read as it was intended to be read—from the beginning to end in orderly and successive progression.

(And to include the **Ex Cathedras** in their likewise proper order.)

ONE integrated and intransigent **WHOLE**.

200

How tenuous a connection (literary) writing has, even at its very best, relative to its full-bodied subject matter.

201

So resist changing my ways, but when forced to, so happy to have done so.